Name _______________________________________ Date _____

Latin in the Christian Trivium
Study Sheet A
Chapter Seven

Grammar

1. What do we call a preposition and its object?_______________________________

____

2. What are the two cases used after Latin prepositions?_______________________

____

3. When motion is expressed, what is the case used with a preposition? _____________

4. If we want to show location or position, what is the case used after prepositions?

____

Practice

Write the meanings of the following prepositions and also the case of the noun or pronoun which is its object.

	CASE	MEANING
5. per	_____________________	_____________________
6. contra	_____________________	_____________________
7. in (acc.)	_____________________	_____________________
8. in (abl.)	_____________________	_____________________
9. trans	_____________________	_____________________
10. e, ex	_____________________	_____________________
11. de	_____________________	_____________________
12. sine	_____________________	_____________________

Sentence Work

13. We are defeating the men of Gaul. _______________________________________

____

14. Because of the wisdom of the men, we are freeing the women. _______________

____

15. In front of the farmhouse the messenger greets the men. ___________________

____

16. The angels do not dwell on earth, but men dwell on the earth. _______________

____

17. Boys carry books to school. ____

____

18. The teacher likes the boys and girls. ____

____

19. He calls the book, *Concerning Nature*. ______________________________________

____

20. Across the road you are looking at the common crowds. ____________________

____

21. Peter is thinking about Christ the Lord. _____________________________________

____

22. The man John is not a slave, but an apostle of Christ. ______________________

____

23. He is in the world, but not of the world. ____________________________________

____

Latin in the Christian Trivium
Supplementary Study Sheet B
Chapter Seven

Tell which Latin preposition you would use for each of the underlined words in these sentences. Sometimes there are two prepositions.   Then tell which case would follow that use of the Latin preposition.

1. He will command His angels <u>concerning</u> you.

2. You will not strike your foot <u>against</u> a stone.

3. Jesus returned to Galilee and news <u>about</u> Him spread through the whole countryside.

4. He went <u>to</u> Nazareth where He had been brought up.

5. The eyes of everyone in the synagogue were fastened <u>on</u> Him.

6. He walked <u>along</u> the road <u>with</u> the disciples.

7. Some of the men were sitting <u>at the foot of</u> the large tree.

8. The hungry men said that they were <u>without</u> food.

9. When Father works, he does it <u>on behalf of</u> his family.

10. The children ran <u>down from</u> the hill because it was so fun.

11. <u>On account of</u> your lovely singing, you are going to study at Julliard.

12. The storm headed <u>toward</u> our city.

13. The storm came <u>into</u> our city.

14. Then the storm headed <u>out of</u> our city.

15. As it blew <u>into</u> Nevada, it was far <u>away from</u> our city.

16. High winds blew <u>over</u> the desert.

17. Put the wood <u>behind</u> the house <u>in</u> the storage shed.

18. We learn Latin <u>with</u> a great teacher.

19. He gave money to the organization <u>on behalf of</u> the blind.

20. We are definitely <u>against</u> wrongdoing.

DRILL SHEET AFTER CHAPTER SEVEN.

TRANSLATE INTO LATIN:

1. under the stars

2. through the forest

3. on account of the common crowd

4. into the eye

5. with the apostles

6. against the nations

7. about the whales

8. behind the farmhouse

9. away from the boys

10. toward the homeland

11. out of Italy

12. across the earth

13. into Gaul

14. out of (from) water

15. on behalf of the family

16. on the tunic

17. among the women

18. between the stars

19. with the boys and the girls

20. against the earth

Latin to English. Translate these phrases and sentences.

21. de provinciā
22. de terrā
23. de iustitiā
24. ad Italiam
25. ad carrum
26. ad magistros
27. ante equos
28. ante raedam
29. ante villam
30. contra turbas
31. contra puellas
32. contra Davum
33. contra nuntios
34. in mundum
35. in mundo
36. in silvā
37. in silvis
38. inter feminas
39. inter raedas
40. ob iustitiam
41. ob stellas
42. per turbam
43. per aquam
44. per Christum
45. per vias
46. post turbas
47. post ancillas
48. post balaenam
49. post discipulos
50. propter sapientiam
51. propter familiam
52. sub provinciam
53. de viā
54. sub terrā
55. sub raedā
56. sub oculis
57. sub equo
58. trans viam
59. trans provincias
60. trans Romam
61. trans Europam
62. trans patrias
63. ab Italiā
64. a patriā
65. a Galliā

66. a turbā
67. a viis
68. a silvā
69. ab apostolo
70. cum magistro
71. cum viris feminisque
72. cum Tito
73. cum viro
74. cum numero virorum
75. cum servis
76. de raedā
77. de raedis
78. de naturā
79. epistula de Deo
80. epistula de ancillis servisque
81. de balaenā
82. de stellis
83. e silvā
84. e tunicā
85. e familiā
86. ex aquā
87. ex aquis
88. e villis
89. ex agro
90. sine iustitiā
91. sine sapientiā
92. sine aquā
93. sine terrā
94. sine oculis
95. pro Romā
96. pro patriā
97. pro Christo
98. pro mundo
99. pro ludis
100. pro Domino

Name _______________________________________ Date _______________________

Latin in the Christian Trivium
Study Sheet
Chapter Eight

Grammar

1. What two cases of neuter nouns are always alike? _______________________________

2. What is the ending of these two cases in the plural? _______________________________

3. Decline **verbum** or **stipendium** and give meanings for each case.

CASE	SINGULAR	MEANING
__________	__________________	__________________
__________	__________________	__________________
__________	__________________	__________________
__________	__________________	__________________
__________	__________________	__________________

CASE	PLURAL	MEANING
__________	__________________	__________________
__________	__________________	__________________
__________	__________________	__________________
__________	__________________	__________________
__________	__________________	__________________

Practice

4. Write the case, number, and meaning of each noun:

    a. Sabbatorum ____

    b. caeli ____

    c. dona ____

          ____

    d. stipendiis ____

    ____

    e. principia ____

    ____

    f. frumentorum ____

    g. caelis ____

    ____

    h. testimonio ____

    ____

    i. dono ____

    ____

    j. periculum ____

    ____

    k. mandatis ____

    ____

5. Write the required forms of each noun or phrase.

    a. toward town ____

    b. in the beginning ____

    c. among the men ____

    d. justice (as direct object) ____

    e. of heaven ____

    f. of wars ____

    g. into Italy ____

    h. under the stars ____

    i. to or for kingdoms ____

j. the lands (as subject) ____

6. Underline the English sentence which is the best translation for the Latin sentence.

a. **In viā est turba.** (1) On the road there are crowds. (2) There is a crowd in the farmhouse. (3) There is a crowd on the road.

b. **Virine bellum parant?** (1) Are the men preparing for war? (2) They prepare the men for battle. (3) Who is preparing for wars?

c. **Putamus de Dei sapientiā et iustitiā.** (1) God is thinking about giving us wisdom and righteousness. (2) We do think about God's wisdom and righteousness. (3) The wisdom and righteousness of God is our desire.

d. **Ubi balaenae habitant?** (1) Where do whales live? (2) Do the whales live here? (3) What do whales have?

e. **Apostoline animos virorum confirmant?** (1) The apostles have strong hearts. (2) Do the men strengthen the hearts of the apostles? (3) Do the apostles strengthen the hearts of men?

Sentence Work

7. *Men love gifts.* The word *men* is used as the ______________________________ therefore it is in the ______________________ case. It is a noun of the ______________ declension, ______________________ in number and ________________ in gender; therefore the ending should be ________; and the complete word is __________________ . The word *gifts* is used as the ______________________________; therefore it is in the ________________________ case; it is a noun of the __________ declension, __________ in number and ________________ in gender; therefore the ending should be ______, and the complete word is ________________ . The word *love* is in the present tense; its subject is ____________, with which it must agree in the ______________ number and the ____________ person; therefore the ending should be __________ and the complete verb is ______________________ .

Translation:____

8. The prophets and the apostles are in Italy. ________________________________

____

9. Do you (sing.) like to look at the games?________________________________

____

10. They are setting the books apart for God's purpose. ___________________________

____

11. The slaves are not the messengers of God, but the angels are. _________________

____

12. The Word of God gives wisdom to men and women. ___________________________

____

13. We love God, because God loves men and women. ___________________________

____

14. Moreover, you do listen to the disciples. _________________________________

____

15. They are in the country, but they do not like horses.___________________________

____

DRILL SHEET AFTER CHAPTER EIGHT

TRANSLATE INTO ENGLISH:

1. e regno

2. in oppido

3. ad Galliam

4. de epistulā

5. sub silvam

6. in bello

7. inter feminas

8. a mandatis

9. ob stipendia

10. ad caelum

11. pro regno

12. de memoriā

13. cum discipulis

14. post villam

15. post oculos

16. pro testimoniis

17. e turbā

18. ex aquā

19. propter naturas

20. pro sapientiā

21. ob periculum
22. de caelo
23. de donis
24. a firmamento
25. sine frumento
26. sine periculo
27. in principio
28. verba discipulorum
29. principium sapientiae
30. principium iustitiae
31. Estis puellae.
32. Non estis pueri.
33. Sunt discipuli.
34. Habito quod habitat
35. Sum discipulus Christi enim puto.
36. Putamus de verbis Philippi.
37. Putasne de verbis Philippi?
38. Puto de caelo.
39. Spectat caelum.
40. Spectas stellas in caelo.
41. Spectamus pueros in ludo.
42. Amo magistrum in ludo.
43. Pueri non habitant in ludo.
44. Numerum librorum portare temptamus.
45. Ambularene temptas?
46. Prophetae poetas in Italiā honorant.
47. Puella feminas honorat.
48. Dat eius *(his)* verbum!
49. Sum beatus quoniam amas me (*me*).
50. Vir enim Sabbata amat.
51. Temptamus enim equos curare.
52. Sunt pericula in Italiā.
53. Puellae autem non laborant.
54. Regnum Dei in terrā est.
55. De caelo angeli gladios portant.
56. Frumenta sunt in carris.
57. Agricola viris stipendia dat.
58. Paramus bellum.
59. Paratis bellum.
60. Paro bellum.
61. Dominus viris feminisque Sabbata dat.
62. Ioannes pro populis mundi lacrimat.
63. Apostoli animum Iacobi confirmant.
64. Dominus viros feminasque mundi liberat.
65. Deus enim mandata dat.
66. Amamus mandata Dei.
67. Mandata populos liberant.
68. Viae ad oppidum sunt.
69. Sunt bella in terrā.
70. Stellae in caelo sunt, non in terrā.

Name ____ Date _____________________

Latin in the Christian Trivium
Study Sheet
Chapter Nine A

Grammar

1. Why do Latin adjectives have three forms in every case? ____________________________

____

2. With what does an adjective agree? ____

____

3. Therefore, does the ending of an adjective always agree with the ending of the noun it

modifies? ____

4. What kind of adjectives may be used as nouns in Latin? __________________________

5. How do we translate **multi** when it is used as a noun? ___________________________

____

6. Complete these vocabulary words, writing the feminine and neuter forms completely.

MASCULINE	FEMININE	NEUTER	MEANING
albus	__________	__________	__________
amicus	__________	__________	__________
altus	__________	__________	__________
beatus	__________	__________	__________
bonus	__________	__________	__________
defessus	__________	__________	__________
ferus	__________	__________	__________
gratus	__________	__________	__________
inimicus	__________	__________	__________
latus	__________	__________	__________

liber

longus

magnus

malus

medius

meus

multus

niger

novus

paratus

parvus

proximus

pulcher

purus

sacer

sanctus

suus

tuus

verus

vester

Practice

7. Decline **patria pulchra,** *beautiful homeland.*

	SINGULAR	PLURAL
Nom.	_____________________	_____________________ .
Gen .	_____________________	_____________________ .
Dat.	_____________________	_____________________ .
Acc.	_____________________	_____________________ .
Abl.	_____________________	_____________________ .

8. Decline **liber sacer,** *holy book.*

	SINGULAR	PLURAL
Nom.	_____________________	_____________________ .
Gen.	_____________________	_____________________ .
Dat.	_____________________	_____________________ .
Acc.	_____________________	_____________________ .
Abl.	_____________________	_____________________ .

9. Write the declension of the following personal pronouns.

SINGULAR   PLURAL

ego __________   **tu** __________   **nos** __________   **vos** __________

__________   __________   __________   __________

__________   __________   __________   __________

__________   __________   __________   __________

__________   __________   __________   __________

10. Write in Latin:

with me _____________________   with us _____________________

with you *(sing.)* _____________________   with you *(plur.)* _____________________

Practice with pronouns.

11. Underline the Latin pronoun which is the correct translation for the italicized word.

a. My friend gave *me* a new dictionary. **(me, ad me, mihi, nos)**

b. Her horse ran *to you*. **(ad te, te, vos, vestrum)**

c. His brother is going *with us*. **(nobiscum, cum nos, mihi, noster)**

d. Give *me* liberty or give *me* death. **(tui, ad me, ego, mihi)**

e. God sees me and everything *I* do. **(me, ego, mihi, mecum)**

f. That was so kind *of you*. **(tecum, vestri, vobis, mihi)**

g. *We* love God's Law for its expression of holiness. **(nobis, ego, nos, vobiscum)**

h. The Lord be *with you*! **(mecum, vobiscum, vester, teipsum)**

i. Angels have not appeared *to me*. **(ad te, mihi, mecum, nostrum)**

j. He has spoken *to you* and your friends as well. **(ad me, ad te, tibi, vos)**

Using Ablative of Means

12. *Pretend you were able to translate these into Latin. Underline any prepositional phrases that would be Ablative of Means in Latin. Two are done for you.*

Example: He did his math homework <u>using a pencil.</u>
He was able to attend college <u>with his full scholarship.</u>

a. We learn about the news each day by means of the radio.

b. Nick became fit by means of daily exercise.

c. Her voice was clear and strong using a new microphone.

d. Rob checked the car's oil with a dip stick.

e. Uncle John wrote *Stone Fox* using his new computer.

Name ____ Date _____________________

Latin in the Christian Trivium
Supplementary Study Sheet
Chapter Nine B

Grammar

Some of you may be wondering where the personal pronouns are for *he*, *she*, and *it*.
You will learn them later again as demonstrative pronouns and adjectives, but you can be
introduced to them now.

	is, ea, id			**ei, eae, ea**		
			Singular			
	Masc.	*Fem.*	*Neuter*	*Masc.*	*Fem.*	*Neuter*
Nom.	**is,** *he*	**ea,** *she*	**id,** *it*	**ei,** *they*	**eae,** *they*	**ea,** *they*
Gen.	**eius,** *his, of him*	**eius,** *her, of her*	**eius,** *its, of it*	**eorum,** *of them, their*	**earum,** *of them, their*	**eorum,** *of them, their*
Dat.	**ei,** *to/for him*	**ei,** *to/for her*	**ei,** *to/for it*	**eis,** *to/for them*	**eis,** *to/for them*	**eis,** *to/for them*
Acc.	**eum,** *him*	**eam,** *her*	**id,** *it*	**eos,** *them*	**eas,** *them*	**ea,** *them*
Abl.	**eo,** *by/with him*	**eā,** *by/with her*	**eo,** *by/with it*	**eis,** *by/with them*	**eis,** *by/with them*	**eis,** *by/with them*

Let's try using them in sentences now. Here are English sentences, and you put the correct form
of **is, ea,** or **id** in place of the blank. Use the English gender; don't worry about translating into
Latin.

Put the proper Latin pronoun in place of the italicized English ones. Sometimes there are two.

    1. Give your money *to him*.   ______________

    2. *He* likes *her*.   ______________   ______________

    3. *She* likes *him*.   ______________   ______________

    4. My friend likes *her*.   ______________

    5. *Her* house is red.   ______________

    6. *Its* coat is soft.   ______________

    7. We will go with *them*.   ______________

    8. *She* found *them*.   ______________   ______________

    9. *Their* hearts were pure.   ______________

10. *To him* we gave the honors.   _______________

This time, substitute in a pronoun in place of the italicized noun; just use one Latin word.

Here are two example sentences:

a. *A good name* is to be more desired than great riches.
   Mentally change to: <u>It</u> is to be more desired than riches.
   <u>Id</u> is to be more desired than great riches.

b. *The rich man* rules over the poor.
   Mentally change to: <u>He</u> rules over the poor.
   <u>Is</u> rules over the poor.

   1. A wise man guards his *tongue*.
   A wise man guards ___________.

   2. The way *of a guilty man* is crooked.
   (Change to: The way *of him* is crooked.)
   The way of ____________is crooked.

   3. The Lord is the maker *of them* all.
   The Lord is the maker _____________all.

   4. The execution *of justice* is joy for the righteous.
   The execution _________is joy for the righteous.

   5. The execution of justice is joy *for the righteous*.
   The execution of justice is joy _____________.

   6. Better is a poor man who lives with *integrity*.
   Better is a poor man who lives with ____________.

   7. It is by *his deeds* that a boy distinguishes himself.
   It is by __________that a boy distinguishes himself.

   8. He offered help *to a woman*.
   He offered help.___________

   9. His friends have gone far from *Peter*.
   His friends have gone far from ___________.

10. The Lord has made both *of them*.
    The Lord has made both ______________.

DRILL SHEET AFTER CHAPTER NINE.

MARK AND TRANSLATE INTO LATIN:

1. the good boys (nom.)

2. neighboring towns (nom.)

3. your friends (acc.)

4. the great commandment (nom.)

5. of pure water

6. to/for pretty eyes

7. in the middle of the island

8. to us

9. true words (acc.)

10. a black horse's

11. Holy God (nom.)

12. of our new books

13. for blessed women

14. evil men (nom.)

15. a pleasing word (acc.)

16. his own school (acc.)

17. with many angels

18. a new commandment (acc.)

19. My friend is a true friend.

20. We honor the memory of your friend.

21. Large whales live near the long island.

22. A man is thinking about his (own) homeland.

23. I am listening to your (pl.) good words.

24. Your words are pleasing to my friend.

25. We are telling you stories about the blessed women.

26. She is singing to the Lord of heaven.

27. A pure girl is pleasing to God.

28. The small book is black.

29. An unfriendly slave is near the farmhouse.

30. The good handmaiden takes care of the small girls and boys.

31. His (own) slave carries the white gifts in a black wagon.

32. We live in a neighboring town in the middle of Gaul.

33. Your words are true.

34. Evil words are not pleasing to us.

35. The apostles are sacred to God.

36. The boys are tall in the poet's family, aren't they?

37. Are there many dangers in Italy?

38. Is the little boy ready to greet the messenger?

39. Because we are free, we are happy.

40. There are many stars in the black sky.

41. The unfriendly men are attacking men in the kingdom.

42. I am asking for a new carriage.

43. The boy is listening to his (own) good friends, and he is happy.

44. A broad and long province is near Italy.

45. The friends are not fierce.

46. Do you like to guard the kingdom?

Name ____ Date __________________________

Latin in the Christian Trivium
Study Sheet
Chapter Ten

Grammar

1. Which cardinal numerals are declinable? ____

2. Decline **duo** and **tres.**

	duo			**tres**	
NOM.	_______	_______	_______	_______	_______
GEN.	_______	_______	_______	_______	_______
DAT.	_______	_______	_______	_______	_______
ACC.	_______	_______	_______	_______	_______
ABL.	_______	_______	_______	_______	_______

PRACTICE WITH NUMERALS

Practice One *Fill in the remaining blanks of this table below.*

ROMAN NUMERAL	CARDINAL	ORDINAL
1. **I**	**unus**	**primus**
2. _______		_______
3. _______		_______
4. _______		_______
5. _______		_______
6. _______		_______
7. _______		_______
8. _______		_______
9. _______		_______
10. _______		_______
11. _______		not given
12. _______		not given

Practice Two *Identify the following as cardinal or ordinal numerals and translate. Use the nominative case unless another case is indicated.*

1. my second report _______________   _________________________________

2. with one friend _______________   _________________________________

3. eight reasons _______________   _________________________________

4. the fourth island _______________   _________________________________

5. with 100 angels _______________   _________________________________

6. four carriages _______________   _________________________________

7. the seventh kingdom_______________   _________________________________

8. two eyes _______________   _________________________________

9. the third language _______________   _________________________________

10. the first disciple _______________   _________________________________

Practice Three *Translate these short phrases into English.*

1. viginti equi ____

2. undecim litterae ____

3. mille viri ____

4. octava causa____

5. nona epistula____

6. decimus vir ____

7. sextus filius ____

8. sexta filia ____

9. primus liber ____

10. quarta porta ____

Practice Four

Translate these sentences from Latin to English, noting use of dative of indirect object.

1. Deus mihi vitam dat.

    ____

2. Christus Filius Dei est.

    ____

3. Angeli nobis de Domino nuntiant.

    ____

4. Agricolae et poetae Christum Dominum amant.

____

English Derivatives

Give 1) the Latin origin for these words and 2) use each in an intelligent sentence.

1. **sinecure**   1)_______________________________

    2) ____

2. **linguistics**   1)_______________________________

    2) ____

3. **copious**   1) ____

    2) ____

4. **ancillary**   1) ____

    2) ____

5. **sublingual**   1) ____

    2) ____

WORD STUDY Write the translation. (Can you count in Latin?)

Una raeda et una raeda sunt duae raedae; duo angeli et unus angelus sunt tres angeli; duo apostoli et duo apostoli sunt quattuor apostoli; tres discipuli et duo discipuli sunt quinque discipuli; quattuor balaenae et duo balaenae sunt sex balaenae; sex mandata et unus mandatum sunt septem mandata; quinque dona et tria dona sunt octo dona; septem gladii et duo gladii sunt novem gladii; sex ancillae et quattuor ancillae sunt decem ancillae.

DRILL SHEET AFTER CHAPTER TEN

TRANSLATE INTO LATIN:

1. eight boys (nom.)

2. five gates (acc.)

3. twenty whales (nom.)

4. seven memories (abl.)

5. eleven messengers (dat.)

6. ten poets (gen.)

7. three towns (abl.)

8. three nations (acc.)

9. nine lives (nom.)

10. nine lives (acc.)

11. the sixth son (nom.)

12. the eighth kingdom (dat.)

13. the first Sabbath (nom.)

14. the second boy (gen.)

15. the fourth man (dat.)

16. the third country (nom.)

17. the third sailor (nom.)

18. the fourth tunic (dat.)

19. the tenth road (nom.)

20. the seventh province (abl.)

21. fama trium virorum

22. quattuor equi

23. septima memoria

24. secundum bellum

25. vitae unius pueri quinque parvarum puellarumque

26. Deus est Unus.

27. mille litterae

28. decimum oppidum

29. tertiā horā

30. Viginti nautae sunt sine curā.

31. Novem servi magni ad villam agricolae ambulant.

32. Virum ob audaciam laudamus.

33. Magister pueris duobus libros dat.

34. Legatus in magnā villā habitat.

35. Quinque feminae sex puellaeque ab agro ad oppidum ambulant.

36. Natura virorum feminarumque non est bona, sed Deus nos amat.

37. Tribus linguis cantamus.

38. Iesus *(Jesus)* discipulis vocat, "Hora adest." (adest = *ad* + *est*)

39. Suntne quinque filii quattuor filiaeque in tuā familiā?

40. Sumus liberi viri liberae feminaeque quod sumus Christiani. *(Christians)*

Name ____ Date _________________

Latin in the Christian Trivium
Study Sheet
Chapter Eleven

Grammar

1. What tenses are formed on the present stem of a verb? _______________________

____

2. How is the present tense of a verb formed? _______________________________

____

3. What is the tense sign of the imperfect tense? _______________________________

4. What is the tense sign of the future tense? _________________________________

Practice. Fill in the blanks.

	PERSON	NUMBER	TENSE	TRANSLATION
5. rogabimus	_____ _____	_______	_____________	
6. sanctificabo	_____ _____	_______	_____________	
7. putant	_____ _____	_______	_____________	
8. portabam	_____ _____	_______	_____________	
9. narrabat	_____ _____	_______	_____________	
10. lacrimatis	_____ _____	_______	_____________	
11. laudabis	_____ _____	_______	_____________	
12. parant	_____ _____	_______	_____________	
13. navigabunt	_____ _____	_______	_____________	
14. nuntiabis	_____ _____	_______	_____________	
15. laboramus	_____ _____	_______	_____________	
16. vocabo	_____ _____	_______	_____________	

Underline the Latin word which is the correct translation for the English.

17. You will strengthen	**confirmas**	**confirmabatis**	**confirmabis**
18. I was taking care of	**curabam**	**curabat**	**curabo**
19. We shall be hard pressed	**laborabunt**	**laboramus**	**laborabimus**
20. They will listen to	**auscultabant**	**auscultabunt**	**auscultabo**
21. They are giving	**dant**	**dabant**	**dabunt**
22. She was honoring	**honorabam**	**honorabat**	**honorabit**
23. I shall relate	**narro**	**narrabam**	**narrabo**
24. I was thinking	**putabam**	**putabat**	**putabo**
25. He used to ask for	**rogat**	**rogabat**	**rogant**
26. He was guarding	**servabam**	**servabat**	**servabant**

Sentence Work. Mark all sentences, and then translate.

27. The second son of the good man used to guard the family.

____

28. The words were strengthening our hearts. (Use **animos** here for *hearts.*)

____

29. Many men honor the Lord, and they will live in heaven.

____

30. The good men will not attack the little boys.

____

31. On a separate sheet of paper write a journal (diary) entry for one of your days this week. You may tell about your family or your school, or what you did today. Begin with "Dear Diary,." **Cara Emphemeris.** W rite it in Latin, of course!

DRILL SHEET AFTER CHAPTER ELEVEN.

TRANSLATE INTO LATIN:

1. we shall praise

2. they were loving

3. you (pl.) are carrying

4. there is

5. you will give

6. you are telling

7. he was telling

8. they will walk

9. she will think

10. we were suffering

11. they are

12. we were crying

13. he is attacking

14. I prepare

15. you prepare to work

16. we like to work

17. he will ask

18. they set apart for God's purpose

19. will you (pl.) listen to?

20. he does announce, doesn't he?

21. I love you.

22. Do you love me?

Name ____ Date ____________________

Latin in the Christian Trivium
Study Sheet
Chapter Twelve A

Grammar

1. What parts of speech do adverbs modify?

____

____

2. How do you change most adjectives of the first and second declension to form them into

adverbs?____

Adverb Work

To refresh your memory, read the following and then do the exercises:
Adverbs answer questions, how, when, where, and to what degree.
     A. Use adjectives to modify nouns or pronouns. Use adverbs to modify verbs,
     adjectives or other adverbs.
          Michael is an *honest* employer. (adjective)
          Michael deals with his employees *honestly*. (adverb)
     B. Use predicate adjectives after linking verbs.
          Douglas seems *quick*. (not *quickly*)
          Douglas runs *quickly*. (answers the question "how")

Underline the correct word in parentheses.

3. After hearing the good news, David became (happy, happily).

4. You must wash your hair (often, frequent) to keep it shiny.

5. Tom is (real, really) fast on the football field.

6. Joe felt (good, well) about performing (good, well) on his new job.

7. Hillarie is (surely, sure) happy about being a mother.

8. We were given Eternal Life (free, freely)

9. He did really (bad, badly) on his algebra test, and is going to make it up.

10. The detective crept through the house (stealthy, stealthily).

Sentence Work

Identify adverbs in the following sentences and tell if they answer the question, (A) *how,* (B) *when,* or (C) *where.*

	ADVERB	WHICH KIND?
11. Brandon will arrive tomorrow.	______________	______________
12. Send all the mail here.	______________	______________
13. Frank answered angrily.	______________	______________

14. The little girl sang sweetly to her tired mother.

______________   ______________

15. Happily, children used the sprinklers to cool themselves on a warm day.

______________   ______________

16. Wise parents stayed at the park where they could carefully watch their children play.

______________   ______________

17. The dogs slept soundly near the warm radiators, seldom going outside.

______________   ______________

______________   ______________

For this part of the exercise, change each adjective below into an adverb.   Then use the adverb in a sentence of your own.

18. kind ____

____

19. fortunate ____

____

20. happy ____

____

Name____Date _____________________________

Latin in the Christian Trivium
Supplementary Study Sheet
Chapter Twelve B

Grammar

Some of you may be wondering where the personal pronouns are for *he*, *she*, and *it*.
You will learn them later again as demonstrative pronouns and adjectives, but you can be
introduced to them now.

	is, ea, id			**ei, eae, ea**		
			Singular			
	Masc.	*Fem.*	*Neuter*	*Masc.*	*Fem.*	*Neuter*
Nom.	**is**, *he*	**ea**, *she*	**id**, *it*	**ei**, *they*	**eae**, *they*	**ea**, *they*
Gen.	**eius**, *his, of him*	**eius**, *her, of her*	**eius**, *its, of it*	**eorum**, *of them, their*	**earum**, *of them, their*	**eorum**, *of them, their*
Dat.	**ei**, *to/for him*	**ei**, *to/for her*	**ei**, *to/for it*	**eis**, *to/for them*	**eis**, *to/for them*	**eis**, *to/for them*
Acc.	**eum**, *him*	**eam**, *her*	**id**, *it*	**eos**, *them*	**eas**, *them*	**ea**, *them*
Abl.	**eo**, *by/with him*	**eā**, *by/with her*	**eo**, *by/with it*	**eis**, *by/with them*	**eis**, *by/with them*	**eis**, *by/with them*

Let's try using them in sentences now. Here are English sentences, and you put the correct form
of **is, ea**, or **id** in place of the blank. Use the English gender; don't worry about translating into
Latin.

Put the proper Latin pronoun in place of the italicized English ones. Sometimes there are two.

1. Give your money *to him.* ___________

2. *He* likes *her.* ___________   ___________

3. *She* likes *him.* ___________   ___________

4. My friend likes *her.* ___________

5. *Her* house is red. ___________

6. *Its* coat is soft. ___________

7. We will go with *them.* ___________

8. *She* found *them.* ___________   ___________

9. *Their* hearts were pure. ___________

10. *To him* we gave the honors. ___________

This time, substitute in a pronoun in place of the italicized noun; just use one Latin word.

Here are two example sentences:

a. *A good name* is to be more desired than great riches.
  Mentally change to: <u>It</u> is to be more desired than riches.
    <u>Id</u> is to be more desired than great riches.

b. *The rich man* rules over the poor.
  Mentally change to: <u>He</u> rules over the poor.
    <u>Is</u> rules over the poor.

Now you do yours.
  1. A wise man guards *his tongue.*
      A wise man guards _____________

  2. The way *of a guilty man* is crooked.
      (Change to: The way *of him* is crooked.)
      The way of____________is crooked.

  3. The Lord is the maker *of them* all.
      The Lord is the maker_____________all.

  4. The execution *of justice* is joy for the righteous. The
      execution_____________is joy for the righteous.

  5. The execution of justice is joy *for the righteous.* The
      execution of justice is joy _____________.

  6. Better is a poor man who lives with *integrity.* Better
      is a poor man who lives with_____________.

  7. It is by *his deeds* that a boy distinguishes himself.
      It is by_____________that a boy distinguishes himself.

  8. He offered help *to a woman.*
      He offered help_____________
          .

  9. His friends have gone far from *Peter.*
      His friends have gone far <u>from</u>_____________.

  10. The Lord has made both *of them.*
      The Lord has made both_____________.

DRILL SHEET AFTER CHAPTER TWELVE.

TRANSLATE INTO LATIN.

1. He was always greeting me.

2. I am not living badly.

3. We shall attack first.

4. Why are there new dangers?

5. Do you often sing?

6. We like to walk to our farmhouse.

7. Afterwards he will heal the slaves.

8. In the evening Peter was telling us *(dative)* about the Lord.

9. He was walking stealthily through the forest.

10. Men often used to think about life, and they were asking God for wisdom.

11. Since we always try to honor our family, we are happy.

12. She was walking through the little town early in the day.

13. Yesterday we were slaves; tomorrow we shall be free.

14. My farmhouse is far away from yours.

15. First, we were listening to the nine tall poets.

16. Were there eleven apostles?

17. He was suffering, but he was always singing.

18. We live on a beautiful earth, don't we?

19. My daughter sings well, and she praises God always.

20. Meanwhile through the forest the messenger was walking.

Name ____ Date ____________________________

Latin in the Christian Trivium
Study Sheet
Chapter Thirteen

Grammar Review

1. The two moods of a Latin verb that you have learned so far are _______________________

____

2. The three tenses of a Latin verb that you have learned so far are _______________________

____

3. The three persons of a Latin verb are ____

4. The two numbers of a Latin verb are ____

5. The present active imperative singular form is the same as the present _________________

6. The vocative case is used for ____

7. The _______________________ case is used to show the duration of time in which

something is occurring.

8. The _______________________ case is used to show the time when something occurs.

9. The _______________________ case is used to show the time within which something

occurs.

10. Who were the three primary pagan gods that the Romans worshipped?

____

11. Why were the Christians persecuted by the Romans? _______________________________

____

____

Practice.

12. Give the present imperative active second person singular of the following verbs.

narro _______________________   **do** _________________________________

navigo _____________________   **nuntio** _____________________________

13. Give the present imperative active second person plural of the following verbs.

ausculto ___________________   **servo** ______________________________

laudo _______________________   **ambulo** ____________________________

14. Give the vocative singular of the following nouns.

amicus _____________________   **filia** _______________________________

filius _______________________   **Davus** _____________________________

15. Circle the Latin phrase that best translates the bracketed English words.

    (a) My friend will walk to my house {within two hours.}

        (1) in duo horas   (3) duobus horis

        (2) duas horas   (4) a duobus horis

    (b) The poet was giving a gift {to the woman.}

        (1) feminis   (3) ad feminam

        (2) femino   (4) feminae

    (c) He was carrying the boys {with the carriage}.

        (1) in raedis   (3) raedam

        (2) cum raeda   (4) raeda

16. Match the English words with their correct meaning on the right.

    1. affiliate   _______   (a) to inspire; to bring out feelings or memories

    2. furtively   _______   (b) everywhere present

    3. benediction   _______   (c) a position or job without anxiety

4. nautical   _______   (d) a nine sided polygon

5. novelty   _______   (e) a measuring device on a plane to determine height

6. approximate   _______   (f) to associate with someone as if your own child

7. pulchritude   _______   (g) stealthily

8. verbose   _______   (h) something new, a new idea

9. convocation   _______   (i) beauty

10. ubiquitous   _______   (j) having to do with sailing

11. altimeter   _______   (k) nearly

12. sinecure   _______   (l) a blessing, "speaking well"

13. nonagon   _______   (m) wordy

14. evoke   _______   (n) the act of calling together a group of people

Sentences

17. Non multis verbis discipuli viris de periculis narrabant.

____

18. Boni amant bona.

____

19. Mali mala amant.

____

20. Defessi ad villam esse amant.

____

Latin Composition

21. On the following lines write a story in Latin of two paragraphs. Each paragraph must have three sentences. Give your composition a Latin title.

NAME ____ DATE ____

1. Ambula, amice, quattuor horas.
2. Ambulate, viri, quattuor horas.
3. Ambula, mi fili, ad meam villam.
4. Ambulabisne ad meam villam quattuor horis?

5. Pura, mea filia, de Deo, et tum canta.
6. Puto, mea filia, de te et meo filio.
7. Putate de mandatis Dei nunc!
8. Putate de mandatis Dei semper!

9. Da dona amico tuo primum.
10. Dabamus dona nostris amicis saepe.
11. Dabimus dona discipulis quod sunt boni.
12. Date, servi, bona dona puellis puerisque.

13. Ubi est firmamentum caeli?
14. Ubi erant inimici?
15. Ubi est ludus?
16. Ubi est liber legati?

17. Postea ambulabitis.
18. Tantum ambulare amant.
19. Equus diu ambulabat.
20. Ubi es? Sum hic.

21. Diu ibi habitabam.
22. Tunc ambulabamus ad insulam.
23. Vocate pueros.
24. Voca pueros.
25. Specta puerum in villā.
26. Spectatisne puerum?
27. Specto puerum.

28. Da, amabo, librum mihi.
29. Da, amabo, librum nobis.
30. Dabo vobis librum.
31. Dabo tibi librum.

32. Unā horā navigabimus.
33. Duo horas navigabimus.

34. Septem annos viri pugnabant.
35. Septem annis viri navigabunt.
36. Quinque annos laborabamus.
37. Quinque annis in caelo erimus.

WORD SEARCH

Circle the Latin words for the English expressions listed below. The words may be read vertically, horizontally, or diagonally, in any direction.

1. war
2. hour
3. book
4. far
5. to
6. early in the day
7. teacher
8. pleasing
9. then, at that time
10. island
11. because
12. good
13. sword
14. with
15. God
16. in the middle of
17. I like
18. I live
19. eight

```
B E L L U M O C O T
C B I O R A C U M M
U Q B O N U S I A E
L U E F D G E N G D
H O R A E L E R I I
A D O M U A N I S U
B O T A S D O C T S
I M A I T I M B E S
T A B X S U T A R G
O I S D T S M A P P
I N S U L A O C T O
```

Latin in the Christian Trivium
Study Sheet
Chapter Fourteen

Grammar

1. Does an adjective of the first and second declension always agree in case and number with the

third declension noun it modifies? ____

2. What two cases of neuter nouns always have the same ending? _____________________

____

Practice

3. Write the requested forms in Latin.

		CASE	NUMBER	LATIN WORD
a.	judge	acc.	sg.	___________________________
b.	doer, maker	abl.	pl.	___________________________
c.	ruler	nom.	pl.	___________________________
c.	man	nom.	sg.	___________________________
e.	ruler	dat.	pl.	___________________________
f.	father	acc.	pl.	___________________________
g	madness	acc.	sg.	___________________________
h.	wages	dat.	pl.	___________________________
i.	soldier	abl.	pl.	___________________________
j.	bravery	gen.	sg.	___________________________
k.	fullness	abl.	sg.	___________________________
l.	king	nom.	pl.	___________________________
m.	salt	nom.	sg.	___________________________

n. name abl. sg. ___________________________

o. brother acc. pl. ___________________________

p. peace abl. pl. ___________________________

q. wife nom. pl. ___________________________

r. will gen. sg. ___________________________

s. sister acc. pl. ___________________________

t. strength nom. pl. ___________________________

4. Underline the correct translations of these sentences.

 a. **Homo puero mercedem dabat.**

 1.) The boy gave the man his wage. 2.) The man will give wages to the boy. 3.) The man's son gave him rewards. 4.) The man was giving the boy a reward.

 b. **Principis filius filiam iudicis amat.**

 1.) The judge loves the son and daughter of the ruler.   2.) The son of the ruler loves the judge's daughter. 3.) The daughter loves the ruler, the judge's son.   4.) The son chiefly loves the judge's daughter.

 c. **Eratne tuum nomen Davus?**

 1.) Why did he name you David?   2.). Was David your name?   3.). Your name is David, isn't it? 4.). Did you know the man David?

5. Underline the Latin words which correctly translate only the italicized word.

 a. Rulers praise *laws*.

   legem leges legibus legum legi

 b. Mothers love *daughters*.

   filiae filiabus filiis filias filiis

 c. There is a great *number of soldiers* in Gaul.

numerum militum   numerus militibus   numerus militum

d. Our ruler is a maker *of good laws*.

bonarum legum   boni leges   bonas legas

Sentence Work Translate these after marking them properly.

6. The student was thinking about the reward.____

____

7. The judge was a student of the law for a long time.

____

____

8. The bravery of my brother was saving our family.

____

____

9. A soldier for Christ thinks about the law and about peace under God.

____

____

10. A man is happy, because his wife is a good woman.

____

Practice with vocabulary

11. About 70% of English words are derived from Latin words. You have probably recognized many already. Circle the Latin root that you see in these words and then underline the correct definition of each. You may use the dictionary if needed.

    a. pulchritude 1) obesity   2) daughter of a viscount 3) physical beauty   4) a mental condition

    b. patriot   1) incompetent   2) martyr   3) hallucinogen   4) loyalist

    c. equestrian 1) dancer   2)   pianist   3) horseman   4) acrobat

d. verbiage   1) trickiness   2) wordiness   3) subtlety   4) codification

e. convocation   1) an assembling by summons   2) meeting quite by chance   3) a
                 fortunate or providential coincidence   4) partnership

Latin Composition

12. On the following lines write a story in Latin of three paragraphs. Each paragraph must have

three sentences. Give your composition a Latin title.

____

____

____

____

____

____

____

____

____

____

____

____

____

DRILL SHEETAFTER CHAPTER FOURTEEN.   TRANSLATE INTO ENGLISH:

1. corpus magnum

2. corporis magni

3. iudex altus

4. iudicis alti

5. iudicibus altis

6. plenitudo pacis

7. princeps nomine

8. miles albus

9. militum nigrorum

10. factor lucis

11. factor bonae legis

12. furor malus

13. furori fero

14. uxor pura et pulchra

15. uxores bonae

16. beata mater

17. beatis matribus

18. principes proximi

19. Princeps est paratus.

20. Mater est mea.

21. Mater est defessa.

22. Patria erat lata et longa.

23. Da militibus mercedes.

24. Da mihi mercedes.

25. Date, viri, meae matri mercedes.

26. Rex est iudex, et est meus pater.

27. Tuae leges sunt verae.

28. Da, amabo, mihi salem.

29. Hominis virtus est magna.

30. Bonus rex puram uxorem amat.

31. Erit pax hominibus bonae voluntatis.

32. Erit mala merces hominibus malae voluntatis.

33. Animi nostri sunt mali.

34. Sed amamus esse filiae et filii Dei.

35. Et amamus esse fratres et sorores in Christo.

36. Homines Galliae magni sunt.

37. Homines Italiae parvi sunt.

38. in medio agro, in mediā silvā, in medio oppido

39. fortitudo hominum

40. cum corporibus

41. sine tuis fratribus, cum nostris sororibus

42. corde magno

43. In mediā insulā erat parva villa.

44. In Galliā diu erimus.

45. sub villā, in viā

46. pax per Christum

Latin in the Christian Trivium
Study Sheet
Chapter Fifteen

Grammar

1. In what case do **-i** stem nouns which are masculine or feminine show the **-i** in the stem?

____

2. In what cases do **-i** stem nouns which are neuter show the **-i** of the stem?

____

3. Name the eight irregular adjectives described in the lesson.

____

____

Vocabulary Work

4. Fill in the missing information.

NOMINATIVE	GENITIVE SG.	GENDER	MEANING
animal	__________	__________	__________
__________	avis	__________	__________
canis	__________	__________	__________
__________	__________	__________	river
__________	__________	__________	citizen
lux	__________	__________	__________
__________	maris	__________	__________
__________	mentis	__________	__________
milia	__________	__________	__________
mons	__________	__________	__________

			death
_______________	navis	_______________	_______________
nox	_______________	_______________	_______________
_______________	_______________	_______________	bread
_______________	turris	_______________	_______________
_______________	urbis	_______________	_______________

5. Write the declension of:

SINGULAR

Nom.	<u>mors</u>	<u>avis</u>	<u>flumen</u>
Gen.	_______________	_______________	_______________
Dat.	_______________	_______________	_______________
Acc.	_______________	_______________	_______________
Abl.	_______________	_______________	_______________

PLURAL

Nom.	_______________	_______________	_______________
Gen.	_______________	_______________	_______________
Dat.	_______________	_______________	_______________
Acc.	_______________	_______________	_______________
Abl.	_______________	_______________	_______________

6. Decline the following adjective.

SINGULAR

	Masculine	Feminine	Neuter
Nom.	neuter	neutra	neutrum
Gen.			
Dat.			
Acc.			
Abl.			

PLURAL

	Masculine	Feminine	Neuter
Nom.			
Gen.			
Dat.			
Acc.			
Abl.			

7. Give the ablative singular and genitive plural of these nouns.

	ABLATIVE SINGULAR	GENITIVE PLURAL
animal		
canis		
flumen		
lux		
nox		
panis		

Word Study

8. Circle the root word (the Latin part you recognize) in each of the following, and then write a definition for each. You may use your dictionary if needed.

maritime ____

DEFINITION ____ nocturnal ____

DEFINITION ____

illuminate ____

DEFINITION ____

flume ____

DEFINITION ____

aviary____

DEFINITION ____

sorority ____

DEFINITION ____

mercenary ____

DEFINITION ____

lucid ____

DEFINITION ____

militia ____

DEFINITION ____

cordially ____

DEFINITION ____

9. Use three of the words from the previous exercise in original Latin sentences of your own.

a.____

____

b.____

____

c.____

____

DRILL SHEETAFTER CHAPTER FIFTEEN.

TRANSLATE INTO ENGLISH:

1. totus mundus
2. rex mundi totius
3. mater hominum omnium
4. Est pater noster.
5. lux sola
6. bonum nomen
7. neuter puer
8. neutra puella
9. copia aquae
10. Eramus sine aquā.
11. Alter puer est Ioannes.
12. Sunt duo flumina in oppido.
13. Date gloriam Deo soli.
14. Neuter vir erat liber.
15. Neuter apostolus est ferus.
16. Uter apostolus erit defessus?
17. Canium cura erat magna.
18. Est avis sola.
19. Suntne ulla animalia in tuā villā?
20. Suntne ulla flumina in Galliā?
21. Sunt nulla flumina in nostrā patriā.
22. Neque canes neque aves in nostrā villā habitabant.
23. Est turris alta in nostrā urbe.
24. Separabant viros puerosque.
25. Da, amabo, servo panem.
26. Non amo album panem.
27. Est panis vitae.
28. Uter est meus amicus?
29. Uter puer est altus?
30. Utra puella est bona?
31. Utrum animal est album?
32. Nocte navis navigabat.
33. Tua mens est pura.
34. Navigabatis in mari alto.
35. In turre statne?
36. In turre nigra statis.
37. In turre albā stamus.
38. Est nullus mors nobis in Christo.
39. Pax vobiscum.
40. Angelus vocabat, "Pax hominibus bonae voluntatis."

Name ____ Date _________________________

Latin in the Christian Trivium
Study Sheet
Chapter Sixteen

Reminders:

Although the endings do not always match, nouns and their adjectives must be in the
same case, gender and number as their nouns. Always check to see if the noun is an
i-stem noun (it has an asterisk in front of it in the vocabulary) and follow the paradigm
given in Chapter Fifteen.

Here are some examples:

1-32.

	case	number	gender	Latin noun	Latin adjective
big animals	nominative	plural	neuter	*animalia*	*magna*
to white bread	dative	singular	masculine	*pani*	*albo*
black ships	accusative	plural	feminine	*naves*	*nigras*
by/with evil enemy	ablative	plural	masculine	*hostibus*	*malis*

You see that the adjectives and nouns are in agreement but their endings are not always
the same. You do these:

	case	number	gender	Latin noun	Latin adjective
to red fires	dative	plural	masculine		
tall citizens'	genitive	plural	masculine		

neither brother's	genitive	singular	masculine		
all the men	nominative	plural	masculine		

	case	number	gender	L. noun	L. adjective
a large reward	nominative	singular	feminine		
to a pleasing student	dative	singular	masculine		
with a good law	ablative	singular	feminine		
by any name	ablative	singular	neuter		

	case	number	gender	L. noun	L. adjective
all the murders	nominative	plural	feminine		
entire bridges'	genitive	plural	masculine		
unhappy cohorts'	genitive	plural	feminine		
with a black light	ablative	singular	feminine		

	case	number	gender	L. noun	L. adjective
with a bad famine	ablative	singular	feminine		
in the black sea	ablative	singular	neuter		

of the black seas	genitive	plural	neuter		
a black night	accusative	singular	feminine		

	case	number	gender	L. noun	L. adjective
all the murders	nominative	plural	feminine		
only a festival	accusative	singular	neuter		
with no famines	ablative	plural	feminine		
with the other name	ablative	singular	neuter		

Now you figure these out, with fewer clues. Decide which case is to be used.

	case	number	gender	L. noun	L. adjective
for new bridges					
with a broad river					
a fierce leader	ablative				
which fires?	nominative				

	case	number	gender	L. noun	L. adjective
all the enemy's	accusative	plural			

only cohorts'					
with no famines					
with the other name					

Translate these very short sentences.

33. The leaders were voting. Duces censebant.

34. The fire was white.   Ignis erat albus.

35. We were walking on the new bridges.

36. Nulli hostes erant in nostro oppido. No enemy were in our town.

37. Are all the animals in our town dogs?

38. The sea is beautiful, isn't it?

39. Your mind is prepared.

40. Our allies are tired.

Translate these Latin to English short sentences too.

41. Cohortes cum hostibus feris trans magnum pontem ambulant.
42. Mea mens est defessa.
43. Animalium agri erant in Galliā.
44. Manebatis in vestrā nave.
45. Villa parvae infantis est pulchra.
46. Milia animalium erant in Romā.
47. Auscultabasne milia animalium ubi eras in Galliā?
48. Caedes milium animalium erat misera.
49. Caedes milium hominum est misera etiam!
50. Meus canis est bonus.

DRILL SHEET AFTER CHAPTER SIXTEEN.

TRANSLATE THESE PHRASES INTO ENGLISH. USE THIS CHAPTER'S VOCABULARY WHEN POSSIBLE.

1. voluntas Dei
2. voluntatem Dei
3. multitudo militum
4. lux mundi
5. alterius iudicis
6. mater omnium hominum
7. nullus frater
8. neutris fratribus
9. ab utrā sorore?
10. cum altero corpore
11. alterum corpus
12. nulli cives
13. factor terrae
14. factor pontis
15. ullus socius
16. ullae matres
17. omnium fluminum in terrā
18. meus hostis
19. vester hostis
20. vestri hostes
21. milia hostium
22. milia ignium
23. milia canium
24. milia turrium
25. milia noctium
26. milia montium
27. mille montes
28. mille naves
29. mille pontes
30. mille urbes
31. centum sorores
32. viginti canes
33. una pax
34. pax sub Deo
35. tres fames
36. tres reges
37. nullus sal
38. cum nulli sale
38. utrum animal?
39. aliud animal
40. bona mens

41. The large animal is a dog.
42. My father loves my mother.
43. Dogs walk on the bridge with the soldiers.
44. The entire bridge was blazing.
45. When will black birds reach the sea?
46. When will the other birds approach the sea?
47. I love black dogs and white birds.
48. Is there any salt in the bread?
49. The whole cohort is approaching the city.
50. The night is black and there are many stars.
51. He was standing on the bridge.
52. He will stand on the mountain.
53. The allies will stand near the tower.
54. Fire is beautiful.
55. Will you stand on a tall tower?
56. We notice your little dog.
57. Were the students observing the judges?
58. All truth is from God's Word.
59. God is the maker of all things.
60. Which girls are prepared to be wives?
61. Which boys are prepared to be teachers?
62. Which boys are prepared to be sailors?
63. Is he the only judge?
64. Was the famine bad?
65. Are any [of the] men soldiers?
66. Murder is bad.
67. A good judge judges sin.
68. The judge gives the soldiers rewards.
69. Neither boy was staying.
70. Neither animal will withstand the fires.